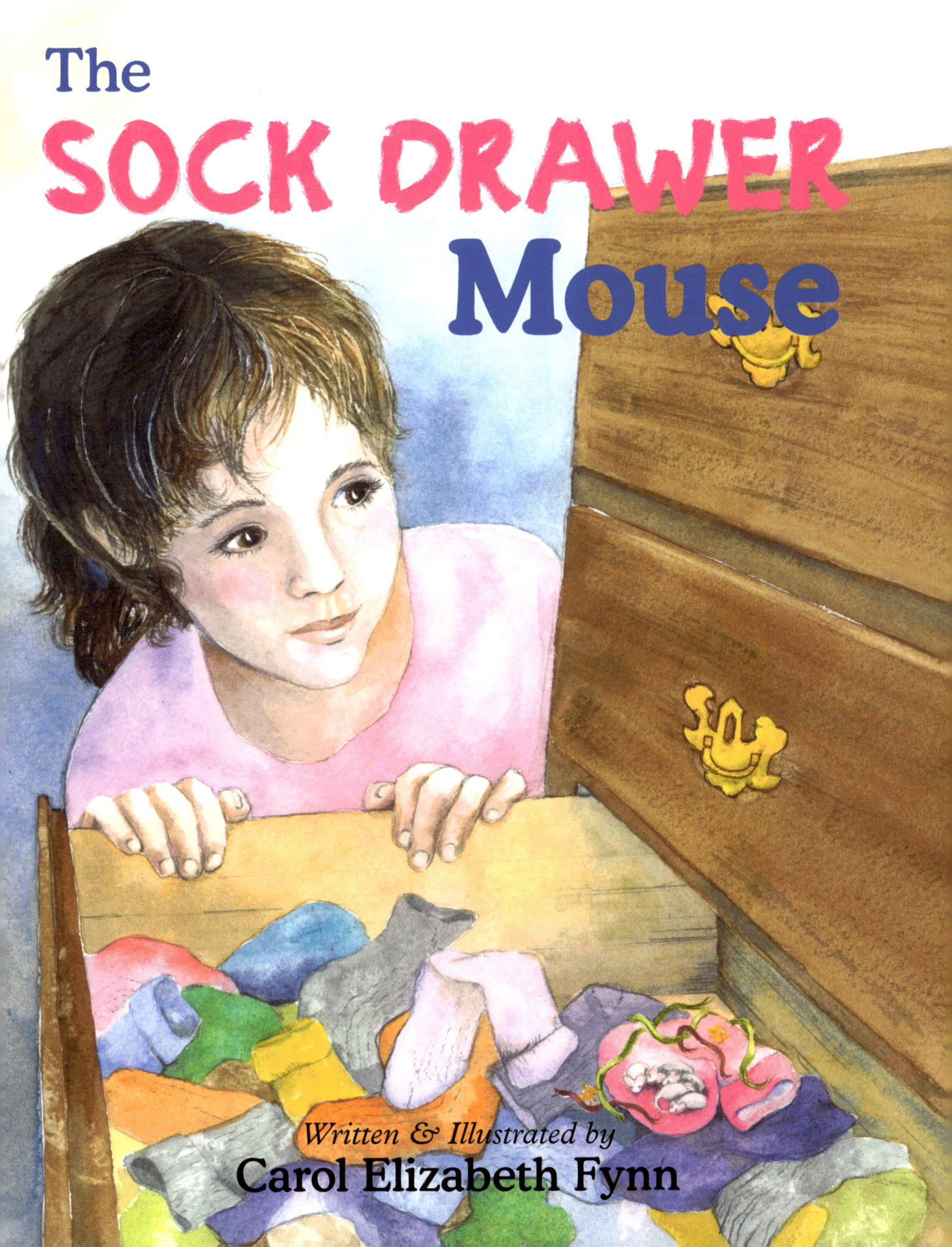

Copyright © 2019. Carol Fynn. All rights reserved.

No part of this book may be reproduced or transmitted in any form or by any means, electronic or mechanical, including photocopying, recording, or by an information storage and retrieval system without written permission of the publisher.

ISBN: 978-1-7332422-1-9

Cover Design and Interior Layout: Ronda Taylor, www.HeartWorkPublishing.com

Illustrations: Carol Fynn. The paintings that illustrate this book were rendered in watercolors, the most fun of all media!

This book is dedicated

To my dear daughter Nicola and her daughter Acadia.

*And to those who appreciate and protect
the wonder of all things wild.*

Acknowledgements

Special thanks to my sweet sister, Melanie, and her daughter, Andrea, for posing for the paintings that illustrate this book.

Furthermore, I am grateful to the generations of students whom I taught at Kirtland High School; they motivated me and rewarded my love of teaching.

A shriek came from Auntie's room.

"Oh no! Awful! Help!"

Not knowing what to expect, Mother rushed in; Nicki followed.

Auntie stood looking into her sewing box filled with embroidery threads of forest greens, lemony yellows, brilliant reds and sky blues. "Oh, look there," Auntie whined. "My embroidery threads are shredded!"

It was true. Some willow greens and sunflower yellows were nibbled into soft tatters. Auntie wailed, "There can be no doubt there's a mouse in the house, and that is very bad!"

Mother teased Auntie by saying, "Perhaps we should move out. What do you think?"

But Auntie's lips grew thin, and she sniffed, "Nonsense. A proper lady shows courage in the face of danger. And we must set an example for the child. Nicki, be brave."

Nicki nodded at her Aunt's command.

That very night as Nicki lay sleeping, it's hard to say what caused her to stir and open her eyes. But open her eyes, she did. And there in a shaft of springtime moonlight, on top of her small dresser was a mouse.

It was a lovely, gray field mouse with sparkling, black eyes and large, perky ears edged with soft, white fur. It sat wiggling its silky whiskers and looking calmly at Nicki.

Most surprised, Nicki gasped. The small sound frightened the mouse who winced and clasped her paws to her chest. She seemed about to flee, but then she showed great courage in the face of danger by continuing to regard Nicki. Silently, Nicki studied the little mouse for yet another moment before falling back into a sound sleep.

At breakfast the next morning, while Mother poured coffee, Auntie sat stiffly in her chair complaining. "More of my threads are ruined," she sniffed. "This time it's the cranberry red. Next it will be my knitting yarns. There can be no doubt there's a mouse in the house, and that is very bad."

Nicki softly suggested, "There are lots of embroidery threads. The mouse only wants a little bit."

Mother gave Nicki a quick look to shush her.

"Nonsense," snapped Auntie. "Threads are necessary to make cross-stitch decorations. A proper homemaker decorates her house tastefully. Remember that, Nicki." Nicki nodded.

Auntie continued, "Something must be done about the mouse. They produce squillions and squillions of babies. The house will be over-run with horrid mice."

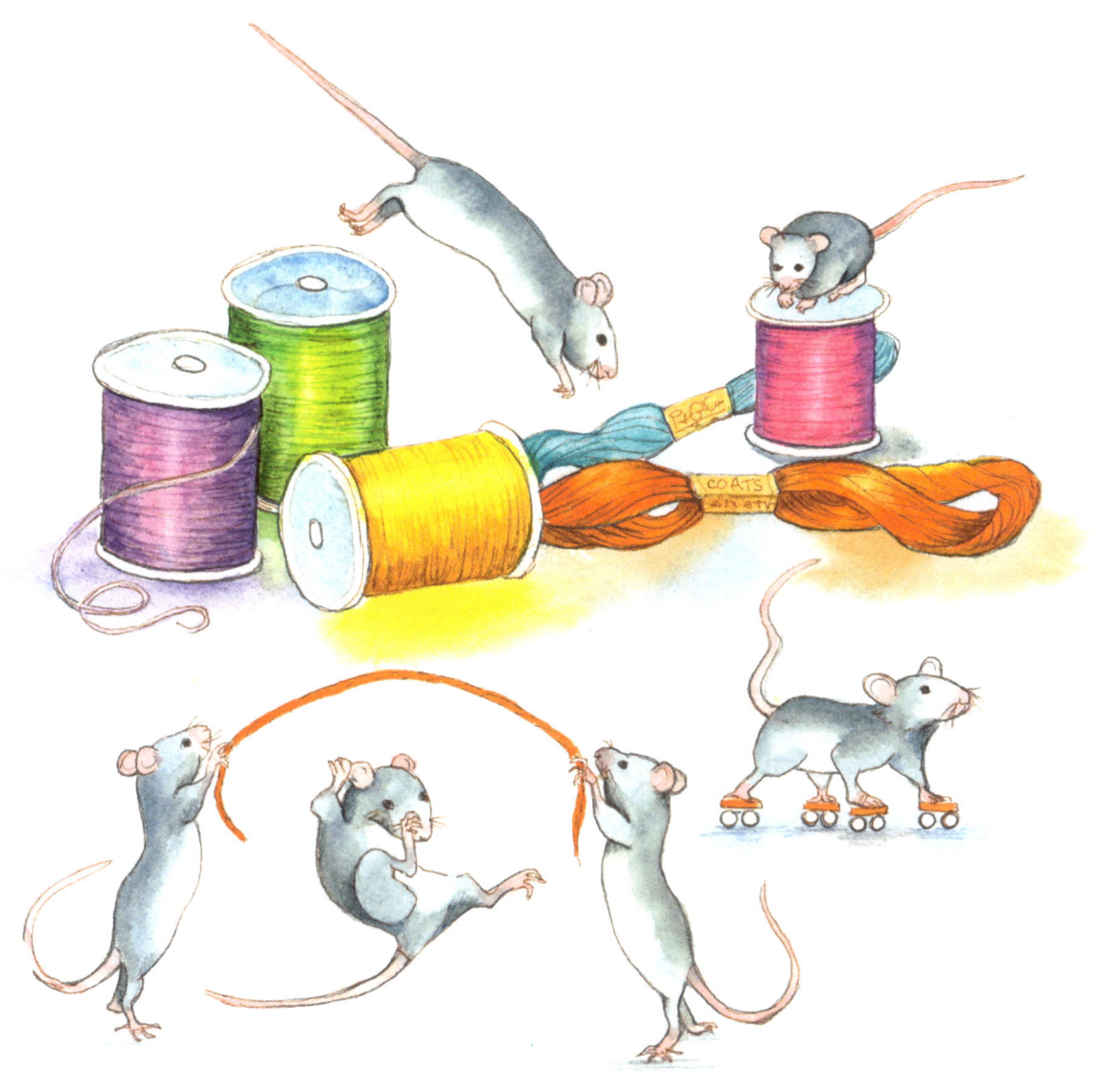

"Perhaps by summer the mouse will move out," Mother suggested.

When Nicki returned to her room to dress for school, she made a most surprising discovery quite by accident. In the bottom sock drawer of her dresser, she found a cozy nest. It was largely constructed from a pair of Nicki's pink cotton socks. However, it was tastefully decorated with threads of willow green, sunflower yellow, and cranberry red.

Nicki shut the bottom drawer carefully. Quickly she dressed for school and hurried out. She had an important question to ask her teacher.

That evening after finishing her grilled-cheese sandwich, Nicki said, "Do you know how many babies a mouse has?"

"Squillions," answered Auntie immediately.

"My teacher says five to eight in a litter."

"Why would you annoy your teacher with such silly questions?" snorted Auntie.

But Mother winked at Nicki and said, "A proper child demonstrates curiosity."

Before going to bed that night, Nicki took peanuts from the kitchen. She tucked the peanuts here and there in her room, placing one on her dresser, one in the wastebasket, and even one in her shoe.

Sure enough. In the morning, as expected, the mouse had demonstrated the curiosity to discover each and every peanut. Nicki was proud of her clever mouse.

However, at breakfast that day Auntie was very cross indeed. She sat glaring at her untouched raisin toast.

"Did you sleep well, Auntie?" inquired Mother.

"Certainly not. I scarcely slept a wink. There were disgusting noises in the night. That horrid mouse was gnawing and crunching. There can be no doubt there's a mouse in the house, and that is very bad. A proper house is a quiet house."

That night when Auntie's snores could be heard rumbling in the dark, Nicki tiptoed to the kitchen to fetch a jar of peanut butter—smooth, not crunchy. She put a scoop of peanut butter on a saucer, which she placed on her dresser. Then she snuggled back into bed.

It wasn't long before Nicki opened her eyes to see the little mouse perched upon the saucer enjoying a fine supper. This time there was no crunching of peanuts. The mouse licked daintily at the peanut butter. She was very quiet—as quiet as a mouse!

Nevertheless, the next morning Auntie was still not happy. She fretted, "We can't have everything nibbled to shreds. A proper family is clean and tidy. And that's quite impossible when there's no doubt there's a mouse in the house, and that is very bad. It's high time we set a trap for that miserable creature."

"Oh no, not a trap!" cried Nicki.

"Just a humane trap that won't hurt the mouse," suggested Mother.

And so it was that a humane trap to capture the mouse was baited with cheese. The slightest disturbance would cause the little door to shut.

It was the teeny, tiny squeaks that woke Nicki in the night. The squeaks led her to carefully open the bottom drawer of her dresser. Snuggled in the comfy sock nest were baby mice—not squillions, just five. With their little noises, the babies called for their mother.

Nicki tiptoed out to the hallway to find her mouse inside the trap cleaning up after her cheese supper. She licked each paw and stroked her fine whiskers. "Very clean and tidy," whispered Nicki as she opened the little door.

Mama Mouse paused nervously and then dashed back to care for her babies.

"You're welcome," whispered Nicki.

Unfortunately, it was Auntie, herself, who discovered the empty trap in the morning.

"Look at this!" wailed Auntie. "I told you! There can be no doubt there's a mouse in the house, and that is very bad. What if that horrid mouse should nibble Nicki's toes? Proper adults protect the safety of their children. The only answer is a mousetrap— a real trap that goes SNAP!"

Nicki grew pale and said nothing at all.

So it was that on Friday night, a trap, the dangerous kind that goes snap, was baited with a delicious-smelling cheese. Nicki was afraid to sleep at all. The moment she heard Auntie's snores, she crept from her bed to the trap. Ever so carefully with a yellow pencil, Nicki touched the nasty trap. SNAP! Nicki breathed a long sigh of relief. All was well for the moment, but something more would have to be done.

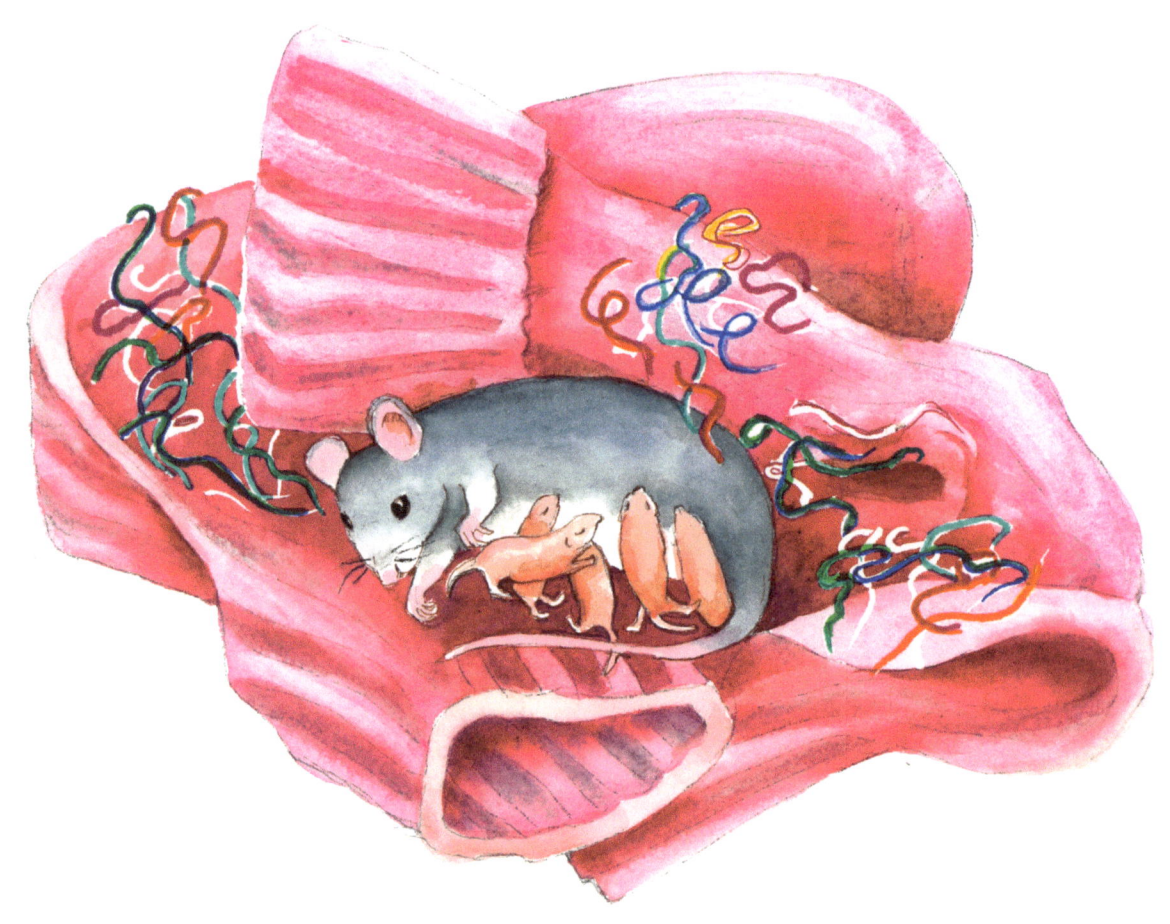

    Nicki returned to her room and peeked into the sock drawer. Nestled in the pink sock was Mama Mouse, feeding her babies. She looked fearfully at Nicki and tucked her babies beneath her tummy. She showed no interest at all in nibbling Nicki's toes. Instead she was protecting the safety of her own children. Nicki formed an important plan of action for the next day.

Saturday morning Nicki was awakened by a shout from Auntie. "Oh no! The horrid thing has escaped. The trap is empty! There can be no doubt there's a mouse in the house, and that is very bad. The answer is traps—more traps that go snap."

Mother nodded. Nicki said nothing at all.

Right after breakfast Nicki excused herself to go play in the garden. But, in fact, she was not playing at all. She was working.

At the bottom of the garden where it was lovely and quiet, and smelled like lilies-of-the-valley, Nicki found a blackberry bush. There beneath the bush in the dark soil, she dug a cozy hole. Down inside she tucked some of her socks. Then she thoughtfully added a good supply of peanuts to last until the blackberries would begin to ripen.

Finally, Nicki tucked in a few strands of Auntie's beautiful embroidery threads so her mouse's house would be tastefully decorated.

Nicki returned to her bedroom and gently opened her sock drawer. Mama Mouse looked up anxiously, but she tucked her babies beneath her furry tummy and did not budge from her nest.

Carefully Nicki removed the drawer from the dresser and covered it with her jacket. She carried it outside to the corner of the garden where she left it beside the blackberry bush.

That evening Nicki was pleased to find that the nest in the drawer was empty. "Well," she whispered, "there are wonderful flowers, trees, nooks and crannies to explore in the garden—enough to satisfy your curiosity. Of course, there are dangers too. But you have the courage to face them."

Several weeks passed with no signs of a mouse in the house, but still Auntie was not happy. She complained about the increasing heat of summer, the buzzing of flies and the sunshine that faded her embroidered cross-stitch decorations. According to Auntie, there was no end to trouble and the house was never proper.

But Mother would just wink at Nicki. And Nicki would smile a secret smile and say nothing at all. For she knew where there was a proper house.

It was right where it belonged, beneath a blackberry bush. And in it lived a perfectly proper mouse.

About the Author/Illustrator

Carol Elizabeth Witwer Fynn was born in Ohio where she lived all of her working life. A graduate of Andrews School for Girls, Wittenberg University, and Kent State University, she majored in English, psychology, and guidance counseling. She studied at Exeter University in England, and did her student teaching in Mexico City.

She is grateful for her thirty-five years of teaching English and psychology, and practicing guidance counseling at Kirtland Schools. She considers it a privilege to have played a role in the perilous and magical school years of many students.

A determined traveler, Carol left teaching for two years to travel around the world to forty-two countries. That challenging odyssey through many undeveloped, remote, and dangerous places gave her a deeper appreciation for America. For the past thirty-six years, she has led groups on annual trips to destinations all over the world.

In retirement Carol moved to Durham, North Carolina, where she took up a new career teaching watercolor painting. She is centered in Durham, but teaches adults in Europe and across the country. She is overwhelmed with gratitude for the opportunities which life has afforded her.

Visit her website at www.watercolorwings.com.

www.ingramcontent.com/pod-product-compliance
Lightning Source LLC
Chambersburg PA
CBHW041412160426
42811CB00107B/1783